Running
on Faith

Running on Faith

Victor Vail

Library of Congress Control Number:		2020914014
ISBN:	Hardcover	978-1-6641-2130-0
	Softcover	978-1-6641-2132-4
	eBook	978-1-6641-2131-7

Print information available on the last page.

Rev. date: 08/06/2020

To order additional copies of this book, contact:
Xlibris
844-714-8691
www.Xlibris.com
Orders@Xlibris.com
815992

Contents

Contents

Chapter 1

Only the Father and I can slope the waters.

A Slippery Slope

———◆———

It started like any other day, most days filled with candor typically do. My mother and I were having our normal morning in the summer of 1996. We were drinking coffee and conversing about whatever came to mind. This was long before Twitter, Facebook, and social media in general. This is when people had conversations. My mother was an unconventional woman. So when she walked back into the little kitchen of our one-bedroom apartment, and she reached for the vodka, it was out of character for her, to say the least; her brother was killed by a drunk driver. She divorced my father because he was allegedly abusive and an alcoholic. So when my mom reached for the booze, it was highly unusual and telling for a woman who played her cards close to the vest; this was a vast ocean of tell. I waited patiently for bad news, but what she said ended up changing my life forever.

"I used to work for a company before you were born," she mumbled under her breath.

My mother stood all of five feet five inches tall but every bit as powerful as a fully engulfed sagebrush fire. Her blond hair was her benchmark; her quiet nature was her saving grace. She could join in on any conversation and handle her own. However, when she engaged in conversation without invocation, that was the real treat.

"Really?" I asked, already knowing she did work for a corporation, but she never got into specifics.

I knew she was a hotel manager, that's what she had done since I could remember, but it seemed she was describing something different. Hearing her engage in this sort of pastime talk intrigued me, so I figured I'd indulge her. She poured her little bottle of vodka in a glass and then made her 125-pound self back into the raggedy kitchen table, which we dubbed the Knights' Circle, and she sat back down.

"What did you do?" I asked.

She took a sip of her drink and chuckled. "I used to put parts and pieces in pagers," she noted and continued. "Manufacturing, I was really good at my job, and I loved it," she added with a shy smile.

As I sat patiently at the Knights' Circle, she continued to entertain me with a time long past. As she spoke, I couldn't help but wonder where all this was going and why she needed the booze. Either way, her next words is the "changed-my-life part."

"I worked at a manufacturing plant until I was seven months pregnant," she said. "With you," she added reluctantly while taking another sip out of her cup.

In all the years, I knew my mother worked but not a blue-collar job like that. Since I could remember, all her employment was, for lack of a greater term, shorthanded, gypsy work. She was a hotel manager and not for the Four Seasons. Her employment at these rundown motels put her in unique closeness with law enforcement. Sometimes she had rough cookies that she had to kick out for not paying their weekly rate, so she kept a .38 six-shooter named Sally, tucked away in her purse for emergencies. Luckily, she only had to show it for real-hard cases so they would get the message. The cops were called on the regular, and they would tell her she was brandishing a firearm illegally. She became fast friends with the common responding officers. She loved the boys in blue.

She continued, "While I was working, I was exposed to radiation. I had just gotten the job not a year earlier, and I didn't want to let them know I was pregnant because then they wouldn't allow me work, per regulations, so I hid it."

She paused for a moment, like she was walking in real time down memory lane.

Then she proceeded, "When the bosses found out, they offered to have you aborted free of charge. Actually, they would even go a step further and offered me money to keep my mouth shut if I did terminate the pregnancy so that later I wouldn't sue them."

"Wouldn't sue?" I interjected.

She took another sip and slowly, almost with a childlike reluctance, then continued, "Well, they said that the radiation exposure, as little as they told us it was, would cause horrible birth defects. They said you'd most likely be blind and you'd be indigent."

She shook her head and added, without second thought, "I said fuck that."

As she stared at me across the Knights' Circle, she continued, "No amount of money was going to let me lose you. I told them, 'If he can't eat, I'll feed him. If he can't go to the bathroom, I'll take him.' I already have two kids out of diapers, and if my baby boy is going to be stuck in one for all his life, I'm the one who is going to be there with him."

I was blown away. Now I understood why she needed that drink. This had been something that had weighed on her chest for a long time. As she regaled me with how my life had started, it all started making sense with how my life was going, and all the odd things that had occurred in my life, up to that moment, started adding up: the continuous resurrection and conversations with a man I call a guardian angel and the intrepid feeling of "knowing," hell, even the all-around feeling of being an odd ball. Everything started coming to light, but fear set me back. I wasn't sure I wanted to brighten what I already knew. I was afraid. But I had to at least take the words she was saying and not try to make them fit at that time but see where they would fall. It felt like a slippery slope.

Chapter 2

How can one see the sun in the sky and believe it is the only intellect?

The Man in the Gray Suit

───◆·◆·◆───

I can't say with accuracy how old I was when I first met Simon, the man in the gray suit, but I was young. The day before Simon and I actually met was a sunny day. I was outside playing in the yard, while my uncle was mowing the grass at our house out in the country that my father just purchased not even a month before. The lawnmower was bogging down on some tall weeds and began to backfire. The sound of the mower drowning in tall weeds caught my attention. So I walked over to see, and as I was watching, all of a sudden, my uncle runs over a rock. That rock came at me with such velocity and smacked me in the forehead; blood flowed viciously. I ran into the house, bleeding all over our new hardwood floors, and my father almost passed out right after I did, so how the story goes anyway. By that evening, I was fine, and by night fall, my head didn't hurt that much at all. By the next morning, everything that had been in front of me was different, visually and physically.

That night, I had this dream. I was on a two-lane road in the desert, walking toward a sunset, and I just assumed it was somewhere in Nevada. As I walked closer, a man in a suit, a tall man, at least six feet five inches, came into focus. He was slender but with broad shoulders, and his grayish-blond hair fell over his gray suit jacket in the back. As his back was toward me, he had one hand in his pocket, and as he turned around to look at me, his face came into focus. His cheekbones were high, and his jaw was strong, and his eyes were filled to the brim with compassion.

"Hi, Victor," he said with purpose and confidence.

I was not afraid of him. I was amazed, not only by the fact I didn't "know" why I was there, but I also "knew" why he was.

Without pretense, he announced very subtly, "My name is Simon. I'm your guardian angel."

His words came from his mouth, so I assumed it was a real conversation. I walked closer to him, staring up at what seemed to me to be a giant in a suit. Behind him, it appeared the last moments of twilight were suddenly starting to become brighter.

He said, "I'll be in touch," and immediately after that, I woke up with chill bumps all over my body. I was very cold, and I knew something wasn't right.

I jumped out of bed and ran to the shower. I was so cold and frail, I could hardly formulate a thought. Looking back, I believe I was going into shock. As I lay in that shower, I prayed to feel better because I wasn't going to wake up my father. Back in those days, you didn't want to involve a working-class parent unless it was literally life or limb. My father didn't have the time, much less the money, to take me to a hospital. I sat down under that hot shower water and prayed to God.

I wasn't a stranger to God or church; my father took me often. He secured a gig at church, recording the service on Sundays and rushing the copies downstairs into the common hall to sell to parishioners. He did attempt to play for the band, but my father was already a musician, and he would often come into church only hours after shutting down a bar. The whiskey on his breath caused the pastor to move him upstairs into the recording booth. My father wanted to serve the Lord in any way that he could, and him being in the recording booth was a 360 win. He could still play music to help his family on Saturday night and record the service on

Sunday morning without insulting the nasal passages of the preacher and still soak in the word. Everybody wins.

I sat in that shower for close to an hour, talking to God, to help me feel better. After I felt like I could at least walk back to bed, I did so in short order. I fell asleep and never saw that man in my *dreams* again. The next morning, I felt his presence, and it was strong. I started wondering what all this means: the dream, the loss of all my energy; and the kicker was that my forehead looked like a pinprick with dried blood, not like the stitch-worthy mess it was just a short twenty-four hours earlier. No one noticed the scar that had taken its place, but I noticed it, and I knew the man in the gray suit noticed me.

Chapter 3

He who created revolutions can also stop a galaxy. We
are here not to indulge but to enlighten those who seek
dark and to brighten those who rush to light.

Stranded

❖

A couple of years after the conversation with my mother at the Knights' Circle that shed light on so many subjects in my life, I found myself in Uncle Sam's war, defending my country, in the US Army. I was flying to all sorts of foreign places, and I was enjoying life, all the while keeping my guardian angel a secret to most. Some knew, mostly family, while others had not a clue, but the knowing part was the real culprit. I didn't focus on it, and it slowly faded. I started to believe that it was just a phase.

As my life began to take shape, I got married to a woman ten years my senior. I was twenty years old, promotable at work, and with a wife who showed me the ropes of how to be a responsible adult. She had three beautiful children from a previous marriage. Mind you, I was only eleven years older than her eldest son. I wasn't stepfather material, more like a cool, big brother. I didn't mind that that's how they looked at me. As time and life moved along, it became more and more difficult to chain down this roving heart of mine. I was being drawn into the next bend in life without fully coming out of the turns I was in.

Toward the end of my stint in the military, my marriage wasn't as strong as I would like it to have been, and I was slowly walking in my father's footsteps with the love of drink. It was difficult all around because of my duty station being overseas. Her children started looking at me with disdain because when we returned stateside, they believed I took their mother away on purpose during the most important years of their life. Even writing these words still pains me. Her ex-husband was not any help as he was helping perpetrate this fraud. However, deep down, I too felt the same way—guilty. At the end of the day, I was a full-blown alcoholic with a music problem. I loved writing and singing but mostly the writing.

As my tour of duty came to an end, late in 2004, my wife's father was fighting for his life. He had suffered a heart attack a week before I got out of the Army. And my wife had rushed to be by his side. A few days later, he was being readied for discharge when I felt the man in the gray suit, Simon, even stronger than normal. I always felt him around, but this time it was with sense of urgency.

I still had three days left at my current duty station, but I felt I needed to be by my wife's side. So I begged my first sergeant to let me sign out early. He smoked me for even asking. (Look up military jargon "smoked.") After I reached muscle failure, he calmly told me to go. "But if you get into any trouble in the next three days (until I'm officially discharged), I don't know you, and I will call you AWOL. Do you understand?" he added with the slightest touch of compassion in his voice.

As I was leaving my military service behind me on that cold night in 2004, the snow began falling. I got on the interstate and drove all night to be with my wife. She was hurting emotionally, but she had to put on a good front of being strong for her mother's sake. I showed up at the hospital around 5:00 a.m. I met my wife outside the main lobby, and she was keeping it together pretty good. It was the day that her father was to be discharged. As we sat outside, finishing up our cigarette, I saw Simon, and immediately, I was to my feet. I wandered aimlessly down the hall, following someone whom I didn't think anyone else could see.

"Am I going crazy?" I wondered.

As I was walking, with my wife trailing closely behind, I was lengthening my stride to catch up with him while trying not to alarm anyone. I followed him all the way back to her father's room. I didn't go in, and Simon disappeared.

"How did you know what room he is in?" my wife asked.

"Simon," I remarked.

We found some chairs to sit in not far away from her dad's side.

The time had come for my father-in-law to be discharged. I went to get more coffee as they were helping get him dressed, and without warning, I felt the chill bumps and the weakness. I felt a presence that can only be described as the last moments of one's femme fatale. I started shaking, and then I heard the loud speaker blare, "Code blue, code blue," and somehow I already knew.

As I rounded the corner, they were rushing my wife's father out of his room. My wife and her mom could not hold back their tears. As my father-in-law rolled past, his eyes were open. I did not see any life in him. Being just out of the war, I knew what death looked like, and for the first time, I believed I felt it. My father-in-law had had a stroke. As they wheeled him, I felt a presence around him, a strong comforting presence. I sent prayers to my angels to please watch over him.

I stood in that hallway only thirty minutes earlier watching him talk, laugh, and love his family. I got out of Iraq with only a scratch when so many of my countrymen didn't make it back at all. My marriage survived my deployments in Europe, and I was to start a new job making $75,000 a year only a week later. I felt I was on top of the world. And here was a man, thirty minutes from discharge from one of the country's leading hospitals, and he had a stroke ten feet away from fifty doctors. He was the blessed one, I thought. He was a lucky one.

He would spend another sixty days in the hospital. Two heart attacks and two strokes later, he was finally going home but not without strings attached literally. The doctors had to put in a heart pump, made by NASA, and he needed a new heart. Troubles were abounding for this family, but somehow I knew God was in control. By March of the next year, he got a new heart and a new lease on life, and my marriage was on the rocks. And to be honest, at this time so were most of my drinks.

For the following year, I felt like I left something in that Iraqi desert a piece of me. I drank myself into oblivion for the sole purpose to be oblivious to life. My wife and I decided to separate. I was glad that my father-in-law was feeling better, and I felt my wife could move on with her life with great large strides. I was truly gracious to the angels that delivered him from the brink, but I hated myself, so much so I contemplated suicide more times than not. I was a wreck, and this glass ship was about to be strewn across the rocks in this ocean we call life. I was stranded.

Chapter 4

Intuition is trust. For only a wise fool will
know all the wrong answers.

Life in the Fast Lane

———◆·◆·◆———

I quietly started reading books on hallucinations and alcoholism.
I scheduled an appointment with the Veterans Affairs office on the East Coast, the same city I was to work in. After that hospital stint with my father-in-law, I felt like I was losing my mind. The VA ran a battery of test. A month had passed, and I had still had not seen a psychologist. I was called back into the doctor's office on Good Friday 2006. The doctor walked in with her eyes glued to the floor, and I knew I wasn't called back there for high cholesterol.

She informed me that my blood work indicated I had tested positive for HIV. (This is the glass-ship-on-rocks part.) My whole life had changed with those five words: "You tested positive for HIV." I was crushed and in a state of panic and disbelief.

How can this be? When did I contract it? From whom? I was married. I gasped.

It wasn't me I was scared for. It was my *wife*. Did I give it to her? Did she give it to me?

11

My mind was a shooting gallery of memories past. But through all the mental chaos, all I could muster to ask the doctor was "Can I still have children?"

"Children?" I thought. I didn't want children of my own—ever.

Until that moment I was quite content playing the stepfather, big brother, friend role. But all that changed in that very moment. This put my wife at a disadvantage because she had her tubes tied. I had to break it to her to get tested, and the VA ran another battery of test on me.

The next two months were a living hell. I prayed, I cried, I cussed out everyone I knew at one point or another. Even cussed out those I couldn't see.

After the last test verified that I indeed have HIV, they handed me a pamphlet and sent me on my way. I remember walking back to my car and sitting in the parking lot. As clear as the pages of this book, I looked over, and there was Simon. He said, "Get a second opinion now."

I drove with urgency to the state health office and sat down with an African American lady. We spoke for at least two hours. The screening part was only a couple of minutes. As she was taking down all my information, our conversations would touch on many subjects that would always segue back to God.

After the paperwork, she took me into the back to draw blood. I didn't want that conversation to end. In the back, there was another lady singing a church hymn while she was putting her gloves on and grabbing her tools. I sat in that chair, scared and visually trembling. I didn't know why I asked, but it just came out. "Do you pray, ma'am?" I asked timidly.

"Every day, sugar," she replied, all the while with a warm, kind smile.

I reluctantly asked if we could pray together. Without any objection or second thought, she removed her gloves, took my hand, and broke into a prayer. For the first time in a long time, I didn't feel utterly alone.

After the test, they gave me a code I would use to get my test results. It would take fourteen days for the results to come back. That was hell. I still went to work, and I had to be strong for my wife. Her blood test hadn't come back yet. Our marriage was hanging on by a very thin, frayed thread.

One day, just shy of the fourteen-day waiting period, it was a Wednesday, I decided to leave work early. I couldn't shake the feeling of despair, and I couldn't handle the stress anymore. It was still two days before my blood test was to be available. I stopped by the store on my way home, and I picked up some alcohol. As I was checking out with my items, I happened to look back to see prayer candles. I grabbed one, not out of necessity, but out of spite. I was truly mad, mad at my life and mad at the world. But above all, I was mad at God. I opened a beer in the parking lot of my apartment. I didn't cry yet. I proceeded to get wildly drunk.

Sometime after 10:00 p.m., that same night, I found myself by active railroad tracks, watching the trains speed by. I felt so far removed from God. I was angry, alone, frustrated, and drunk. I hated myself with a passion, but I was still vain enough not to step in front of a train. I wanted an open-casket funeral. That also served as a clear sign I wasn't crazy, just exhausted.

Just past midnight, I started walking home, and I had screamed to God at the top of my lungs as all those trains passed and still felt no relief. I was rounding the corner on the small road my apartment was on when I passed a closed church. I figured I'd knock and see who, if anyone, was available to talk. So I did. He didn't answer immediately, and I told God that He lied. I told him that it was Him who said, "Ask, and it shall be given you; seek, and ye shall find; knock, and it shall be opened unto you" (Matthew 7:7 KJV). (It is not a sin to remind God of His promises.) I'm not proud of it, but I cussed Him out the rest of the way home.

When I got home, I climbed into the shower and felt that familiar presence again. I was so drunk that as I got out the shower, I slipped on my soaking pants leg and fell onto the floor. There I was half naked, cold, and out of steam. I submitted to that night. I prayed like I had never prayed before and cried myself to sleep on that cold bathroom floor.

The next morning, I got dressed for work, and I was pulling myself together when my phone rang. It was the nurse from the state medical office. She asked me to come in so I could give her my code. My code was the number given at the blood draw to confirm and check the status of my

HIV test. It was against regulations to conduct the check over the phone; it had to be done in person. Nervously, I searched for that tiny piece of paper, but I couldn't find it. I figured that with all of the conversation she and I had, I wouldn't be that easy to forget, but as I was walking out the door, that prayer candle that I bought the night before was still burning strong. As I blew it out, a piece of what looked to be lint was in the melted wax. The closer I looked, it became clear. Sometime the night before, after drinking a considerable amount, I lit the candle and dropped that little piece of paper with the code into the melting red wax. I grabbed some tweezers and pulled out the wax-stained red piece of paper.

I jumped into my car and rushed to the state health office. I waited anxiously in the waiting area when that presence showed up again. Immediately, I was calmer and collected. All the anxiety of the weeks before just disappeared, it was the oddest sensation. Not all the way, but at least I didn't look like a squirrel that just did a line of coke.

She called me back and asked for my paper with the code on it. She asked me what was on the paper, and I told her about the night before and how I found it in a prayer candle this morning. I found out in short order that I was *not* HIV positive, and I cried again. She reminded me about our conversation the weeks earlier and how I made a promise to God that I would start to live my life.

Everything that was my life up to that moment came into focus. The portrait of my life was a sad cry from ideal. I just went through the ringer. Even when I knew I was okay, it felt like my life was over. Looking back at all that wasted time, I needed to make a change, and I knew it had to happen fast.

At this time, my marriage was officially in the ending phase. My wife's HIV test also came back negative. I hated my job, and I hated myself. Somehow God made a way. For some reason, He helped me. His mercy was bestowed upon a golden-hearted drunk. I felt I didn't deserve it. So in turn, I didn't believe I was in the clear. It seemed after that day I started living life in the fast lane while still looking for something in the back seat.

Chapter 5

Fate is falling sand. How can one trust to
know where every grain will fall?

That's All I Have to Say about That.

❖━━━◆━━━❖

A few short months later, I quit my job, started my divorce, and found myself in Alaska. I had taken a job up there to get away from the bad memories. I was still partying any chance I could. Life was becoming a blur, snap shots of memories, but through all of it, I still knew Simon was around. I tried to ignore his attention, but I felt a frequency that made me feel like I was always being judged. So I figured, screw it, I'm a failure. It was like I was looking for a reason not to move on. I was more comfortable with being in my pain versus being optimistic about finding joy in life. How insane is that? It was an immature and dangerous mindset.

I had just gotten a reprieve from the heavens above, but I was still living like I was dying. I was afraid to get attached to people, especially the opposite sex. I was afraid that the state medical office was wrong, so I was ever so careful. I would have to tell the story before anything sexual would happen. Even when they understood, I was extremely careful. It took some time to get back in the saddle, if you know what I mean.

A friend of mine, Jose, and I decided one day to drive to North Pole, Alaska. We spoke about everything en route, and he was the one who actually got me the job in Alaska in the first place. We ran into a group of partygoers up in the North Pole, and one thing led to another. Next thing you know, we find ourselves staring at a bonfire. They started passing a pipe of what looked to be marijuana. I did not partake fully, but I got a buzz. Suddenly, my world and my way got a lot bigger, and I could see colors and hear tones that I wasn't able to comprehend every day. I felt like I was not even real. In short, I was high. We all sat around that bonfire discussing life, death, and love. The reflection of my life at the time all went hand in hand. My ex-wife had moved back with her parents, and I was off yet again in a faraway place, this time looking for myself.

I stayed in Alaska for six months and moved back to Texas to live with my sister. My divorce was final, and I was unemployed. If I was looking for change, I found it. I have not been unemployed since I was thirteen. I was a basket case. I ended up helping my brother with his legal troubles because he had found himself on the wrong side of the law—again. I had a little coin saved up and hired a parole attorney. My brother made parole and began living his life. He found a beautiful girl, Roxy. In the meantime, I landed a job in Kansas, but I didn't have the money to drive up there, much less find a place to stay until I got my first check. The day I was supposed to leave, I was preparing to give up and called the lead man and explained my circumstances, but then, Roxy.

My brother called me first thing that morning and told me he had some money for me. He gave me $500 and a good luck. I didn't know it then, but that moment would change my life forever.

I packed furiously, and I drove all night to get to Kansas to start work the next day. I was exhausted when I arrived, but I was sober. I started working, and a few short days later, my money problems went away. I felt I was finally moving on with my life.

I met someone, Heather. She too worked at the same place I did. We were smitten for each other. She was articulate, bright, and sassy. She was living her life kind of like how I was living mine—feathers on the wind. We started dating, and then just weeks later, she got pregnant with our first child.

That same week, they told many of us that we had to transfer or we would get laid off because of the downsizing. I had a kid on the way and a decision to make. So she and I packed up and moved on.

In the back of my mind, I always worried about my child's health, so much so that every doctors' appointment was chock-full with silent pleas to God that she would be healthy and those second and third opinions were correct.

Shortly after we arrived in our new digs, Heather was hell-bent on getting married. She presented a good argument: She didn't want her first child to be born out of wedlock. So I found myself across the justice of the peace, a mere seven months after my first divorce. This chapter is titled "Life in the Fast Lane." I said nothing about turn signals. I went to as many doctors' appointments as I could, and I tried to be a good husband.

The day my daughter was born was the first day in a long time I was sober for an extended time. We arrived at the hospital at 6:00 a.m. Our little girl wasn't born until 7:24 p.m.

As I stood there watching life in its most natural form, it was something brand new to me. "I have a kid" was all I could think, and she was as beautiful as a summer's sunset.

When I heard her cry for the first time, I remained composed. When the doctors were wrapping her up in her pink blanket, I remained in control. When my daughter's cry subsided, I got worried. I walked over a little closer, and she was staring not at me but through me. In that brief moment, I felt the strongest emotions of love and absolute fear at the same time. Then I cried like a baby, and so did all the nurses. They were crying because I was emotional, and I was crying because I felt that presence, and I could tell she felt it too. I felt she could also see it. That day will forever be sired into my memory.

Our daughter was an angel to me, like how so many other parents feel about their kids. She ignited a spark in me that would never be extinguished.

I didn't change drastically, if any at all. I just responded differently to everyday situations. I wanted to think more kind things and do more kind acts. Ever since I could remember, my father taught me three things: how to love, how to run, and how to be kind. She just magnified all those qualities by a thousand.

We made plans to visit the family back in Texas to show off my little girl. I really wanted her to meet her uncle and aunts. Her uncle was the nicest fella she could know. Her aunt, my elder sister, was more of a mother figure to me when my mom left when I was three and before my mother and I reconnected later. My sister said we could stay with her. Sadly, Roxy passed on before she could meet the little girl she was almost directly responsible for bringing into this world. I found out later that Roxy gave my brother the money so I could go to Kansas in the first place. Roxy passed on five months after my daughter was born, and she never got to see the miracle that was the result of her kind, selfless act.

I cried hard on that rainy night in April 2008. If it weren't for Roxy, I wouldn't have gone to Kansas and met Heather, and Cheyenne would've never been born in Pennsylvania. My life was a geographical oddity of coincidences that were too many to count. We will explore that later. But for now, that's all I have to say about that.

Chapter 6

Only through faith. Even when you can see only faith. Chosen hearts are not chosen to live abundantly. But are chosen to translate to others how to find a life of abundance.

Weak Vertebras

———◆·◆·◆———

After the death of Roxy, everything seemed to fall apart. My brother was shaken to the core and found himself back in jail. Roxy was my brother's best friend, and when she passed, depression and bad decisions drove him into a pretty dark corner.

I was back in Texas with no job, and I had my wife and a little girl to support. I thought my marriage was okay, but my wife, on the other hand, wanted to move back with her mother, and I was having problems coping with society.

It was a cool day in June that everything for me disintegrated. When my sister and Heather decided to go get a bottle of bourbon, I knew, on this cool night in June 2009, it was a mistake, but I assumed, I guess it was through faith, that this night needed to happen. My daughter was asleep, and my wife, sister, and I were drinking. Both of them are Veterans as well.

Neither of them has seen a real war zone, only on a globe, and they were critical of us who have, saying things that, in hindsight, were said to set me off, I believe. They were saying things like "All of you were used for Bush's proxy war, and that's why we stayed in the rear because were not stupid. You were dumb enough to follow those orders," and on and on they would go.

Do you know dissociative disorder? Blacking out on rage and whiskey are two different things. In short, I didn't spend a minute in the "drunk tank."

The last time I saw my little girl was that night in June. I became enraged, erratic, and destined to let this all hit the fan. Emotions of frustration boiled over.

We had had lived in this two-bedroom apartment with my sister, her boyfriend, my wife, sometimes my sister's two almost-grown kids, and my daughter, and we weren't the Waltons. In short, we were all in one another's faces all the time. It was a powder keg. Hard times were the flint, the Bourbon was the gun powder. (I never even had a sip of the Jack Daniels).

Then to add on, I was the only one bringing in any reasonable income, and these two, my sister and Heather, were talking crudely about those who went to Iraq. I yelled, I screamed, I hit the wall, and I left.

When I came back, I was greeted by two police officers. I remember my wife, Heather, holding my daughter under a streetlamp as the police handcuffed me.

The last image I remember was seeing my daughter wave at me through the cage glass as I sat in the back of that police car. I was right where I needed to be. Mission accomplished.

Charged with assault, family violence, second-degree felony, I found myself within the peaceful walls of the county jail. I was in segregation, and I loved every minute of it. I was alone, but I wasn't. Simon was never far off. I found many questions and answers being put on my heart. I cried a lot, and I died a lot. I had gotten a tattoo on a trip to Vegas that read "Only death will set me free." In short, dying to self was the only way to begin to start living for God.

After ten days, I got out of jail and was able to return to live with my sister. My child was gone, my wife was gone, and my car was gone. I again had lost it all and facing some serious jail time.

Then at the end of my rope, the judge told me that I was to complete a full evaluation from the VA. If I failed to show up for any appointment, he would revoke my bail and issue a warrant. The only problem I had with that was the VA told me some years back that I had an awful disease. I was in fear to go back to the VA but not afraid of jail, and once I realized that I thought jail was better than the VA, it was all the writing on the wall I needed to see to know I needed help from the VA more than ever.

I began taking classes at the VA. It was slow going at best. More frustrations, more anger, more Simon. Slowly, my heart was being pulled into an abyss of the unknown. Instead of steering away from the dark, I realized I had to go through it. I couldn't steer clear of the darkness. I had to go through it and bring the dark things back with me into the light. In short, I needed to give life a chance again.

I met a psychologist, and he psychoanalyzed me down to a science. The more I opened up, the more I realized how lost I was. Frustration of the war, anger because someone's mistake almost caused me to question *everything*. He delved into my life, my past, childhood, and military service. Nothing was safe from discussion. I told him the truth. How my childhood was awesome from the time I could remember. My father was a "Rolling Stone" playing music in bars. And I was my father's roadie. My father still drank, but he left the hard stuff alone. My father was my best friend, and I was his. My doctor asked me for a backstory, so here it is.

My sister had moved out when I was eleven and started her life, and sadly, my brother was in jail. So it was just my father and me. He was never abusive, but when I got older, he did show who ran the roost. But whose father doesn't when one becomes a teenager? My father asked, not demanded, respect. I loved my father, and I gave him the respect he deserved. He worked hard to keep a roof over my head when he was on the road for weeks at a time. I always went to school and did what I had to do to not stress him out in any way.

The doctor and I touched on my marriages. I had to come to grips with the fact that my shortcomings were not always mine alone. Still, I missed my daughter and wife.

It was Christmas 2009 that divorce papers found me, yet again, with a catch. That I give up full custody of my daughter, so I thought. I didn't even read them. I knew they were on the way. I waited for the mailman, and by the time he stuffed the other mailboxes, the divorce papers were signed and back in an envelope. According to the law, I wasn't my firstborn's father anymore. To be honest, I just gave up the fight. That's hard for someone who usually carries a chip called the world on his vertebrae.

Chapter 7

Walk fourth in hope, the cousin of faith.

Say a Prayer for Me

———◆◆◆———

As I sat in my doctor's chair one day, we'll call him Victor, it was closer to the end of our time because my deferred adjudication from the judge lasted seventeen months. We were talking about life and just summing up the session, and I asked him if he had any kids. Was it inappropriate? Maybe, but I wanted to know a little more about the guy who knew everything about me. He answered that he and his wife were unable to conceive. I felt like a piece of shit. Here was a man who dedicated his life to help others and unable to have children, and on the other end of this spectrum, there is me, a drunk, almost faithless piece of human excrement. That's how I felt at the time.

In the following months, I was prescribed medication and completing my deferred adjudication sentence. Relationships were sporadic at best until I met Brandy. It was a quick courtship, a fast pregnancy, and an even faster breakup. But in that, we had a little girl. We knew that she and I wouldn't work out, but we made it work out the best for our child. I wasn't much of a father yet. You know those roads in Any Town, USA, that it seems are constantly being worked on? Well, that was my life, same road, different kinds of construction and deconstruction all the time. I hardly saw my second daughter and had yet to see my firstborn since the night I saw her underneath that streetlamp. The memory of being in the back of that police cruiser was slowly making its way into the potluck party of my regret and pride. Lord knows what would show up next.

I got close to Victor and I respected him. I enjoyed my sessions with him a lot. I saw the same kindness in him that I saw in Roxy and my daughter's eyes. He gave me sound advice, I valued his honesty, and at times I hated him for the same reason. Even though I was drinking and occasionally smoking marijuana, I was not seeing, but feeling something different, a presence unlike Simon, even though Simon was always there. No, this was much stronger, more of a purpose. That was this driving force I had yet to officially meet.

I remember I started having vivid dreams at first. Then I started seeing those dreams come to fruition, i.e., say you dream something, and in the next days, that familiarity of a dream comes to pass. It was just like that but all the time. Not that I could see the future, but I was always just a little time removed from it. It was in these days that whatever I tried not to pay attention to earlier in my life was knocking at my door. I knew it was a matter of time before I would have to really open up.

I shared these events with Victor and asked him one time if I was crazy. He said a firm "I don't think so, but who knows?"

At one of my meetings with Victor, I brought a little story for him to read. It was only twenty pages, and it was a story that stretched over a twenty-four-hour period of my life. I titled it "Running: Diary of an Alcoholic, Memoirs of a Madman." His review was short: "It was deep" were his exact words. He never gave it back to me.

I told Victor about my life for almost two years. In that time, I still knew only very little about him. He diagnosed me with PTSD. Again, I felt sorry for myself, but I was pulling my life together.

During this time, my sister and I started a cleaning company. I was working four days a week, so I wasn't drinking that much. I still wasn't a father to my child, but I was dating someone on a serious level. She had a son, and suddenly, I was back in the stepdad-friend mode.

Her son, Jeremy, was a good kid, new-age hipster type and a gamer. He had a circle of friends that loved him, and that was great. Unfortunately, his mom didn't take our relationship as serious as I did, but I wanted the best for the both of them. It wasn't long before colors of convenience started to shine. At one point, I loved her deeply. I was just not in love with her. We soon broke up, and I was living out of my suitcase again. Her son had joined the Army as an aviation mechanic, same job that I had. I was proud of him, and his mom and I were still close. She and I often would pray together. We understood that we weren't good for each other, but we were great for each other. That kind of understanding between wanting souls is rare.

One day, as I sat waiting for the bus to take me to see my doctor, Victor, at that bus stop, I felt Simon again, and a dream that I had the night before came flooding back. I remembered a dream of high clouds, surrounded by a golden wall of further clouds afar, and everyone was happy. But that feeling of the presence was different, more remorseful, not strong but like a pillar. Something this time was wrong.

As cars were passing by, I had to ease my mind, but it was futile. A phone call broke my concentration. It was the doctor's office. The secretary on the line was polite, too polite. "Remorseful," I thought.

I thought I was running late. She said I wasn't and please don't come in. "Why?" I asked.

Truly stumped, she informed me that Doctor Victor was killed by a drunk driver two days prior. I was weak. I asked stupidly, "Are you sure?"

I could hear her hold back a sob, and I knew right then and there that the man with whom I shared so many pieces of my life and who filled in the blanks when I couldn't was gone.

I sat at that bus stop still wreaking from the night before, and the man I considered a confidant lay in repose, killed by a drunk driver. My world slowed to a crawl. I walked back to my apartment and crawled into bed.

I thought about those clouds of gold as I lay there. "What did that mean?" I contested out loud.

My mind raced with possibilities of what it could mean. That presence was ever close. I spoke out loud, "If you're not of Christ, leave." It stayed.

All I could do was lay there, sad, humbled, afraid, alone, but I wasn't. That day was the start of something bigger than me.

After that day, after I lost whom I considered to be a friend, I chose not to fall, not to feel sorry for myself, and above all, not to be mad at God.

"Now that my potluck of self-deprecation is complete," I thought, "time to take it in and keep moving."

And then it became abundantly clear, clearer than when I saw Simon, as clear as you are seeing these words. I said a prayer for Victor, and I asked him to say a prayer for me.

Chapter 8

Hearing words of the wise scares a fool.
Hearing a fool vent scares the wise.

A Brother's Love

A series of leftover regrets, blind turns, and right roads led me to a place of crazy peace. I say crazy peace because my body was calm, but my mind was without stopping. I had to learn everything I picked up. I had to drown that craziness which was my mind. All the while, I was growing closer to Simon and the other one. I couldn't "talk" to the other one. When I did start talking to it, it was slow going at best. Imagine that you try to send a message to Jupiter in Morse code. That's how slow the presence operated. More on that later. But Simon was all ears, it seemed.

For a while, there wasn't a problem I couldn't handle. I met someone new, and we had a child, a boy. Like I did with my other children, we gave him a strong name. I called him the name of a buddy who died in Afghanistan, Clint. Clint was a hell of a pilot and an even greater friend. I always want to remember him and how he died fighting for our freedom. And believe me, freeing the oppressed was our motto. Every time I look at my son, I think of the brave souls who perished that day, and all the days in a war that seemed to have no end. And without hesitation, I was arrested again shortly after my crazy peace.

I spent a year waiting on a court date that never came. I was in a one-bedroom shack living day to day on one-room regulations. I couldn't leave the state, and I was going stir crazy. I needed a change, and I needed one quick. It was in June 2012, a change a cometh. I called my sister because I needed money to get out of town. She coldly told me to ask "my God." At first, I felt as if she was mocking me. I sat in the doorway of that bedbug-infested motel, happy because the case was dismissed and I was free, rightfully so. It was still five days before payday, and I was impatient. Then it happened, I calmed myself, and I prayed to God to help me. I just wanted to feel the road beneath my feet like the old days with my father. Then there was a kind soul named Charlie. I was sitting in the doorway, and he approached me and asked for a cigarette. I obliged, and we started a conversation. Charlie was from Nevada, and he was stranded here in Texas, trying to get back. He needed a cheap ride back to Nevada, and I needed money to leave town. He had to go try and pick up a check, and I had no gas and no money. Decision time.

I had the hotel room until Wednesday morning, payday, but I had no gas and no money to take him fifteen miles away before five so he could pick up his check. So I took a major loss, and I asked for a refund for my room. I was going to check out and use the money to get gas to get him to get his check. We made a deal that if he fronts me the money until payday, I'll give him a ride, and I'd pay him back the cost 50/50. We didn't make it in time to pick up his check, but Charlie was guaranteed he could pick it up Monday morning. Time to make another hard call. I could go back to the hotel and get a roof, but I was too broke to buy food, or I can take the $30 they refunded me to get food for Charlie and me for a couple days, and we can just camp out in my car under the bridge. In the end, I wasn't helping Charlie. He was helping me, and he too had been through a lot in his life, but he handled everything with compassion and regard.

That Monday morning, we were on the road. It was a journey, a brand new start. I felt the change coming.

We made it into the deserts of Nevada at about 10:00 p.m. on a Tuesday. I was tired, but hope for change is a driving force. We stayed in a town called Goldfield for the night. I wasn't going to drive around Area 51 during the night.

As we were laying it down for the evening, Charlie looked at me and said, "You're an angel. Thank you for taking me back home."

I was caught off guard. I never set out to be a changing force. It just ended up that way. Those simple words Charlie spoke changed my life that night. All of a sudden, I gave positive thought to the fact that I might make it through yet.

We slept for a couple of hours, and then we were back on the road. My vehicle never missed a step, and I dropped Charlie off in Reno. As were saying goodbye, I instantly knew I wouldn't see Charlie again.

You see, through all the miles we traveled, we spoke about life, death, and love, my wheel house. But quickly, he offered something else: hope.

We spoke about hope, and Charlie confided in me that he had AIDS. We prayed together down many miles. He was going home to be with his brother. For almost every mile, I prayed for the same grace that God bestowed upon me to be crowned upon Charlie. I felt for him, and I was sad, but he was glad for me to help him, and he was happy. As I left Charlie's apartment complex, I spoke out to Simon.

I was beside myself that just with a kind act to help another, it changed my life for the better in the same swing. I drove all the way out to the Pacific, the Blue Majestic. I sat in awe of the scale of such magnificent beauty, and until that day, God's graces only seemed like a pinprick. It wasn't until that day that purpose and a brand new plan was on the agenda. I felt the presence of something different, and it wanted to get my attention.

I was sober for days at a time. I was driving, so I had to be. Over the course of thousands of miles, I started speaking out to God almost all the time, Simon too. I became more giving, understanding, and patient. I was still taking medications, also reaching out into the good book, not as much as I should, but more than I usually do. And then again, I thought, "I might make it yet."

The running finally led me to settle in Oklahoma. Why Oklahoma? Because there, no one seems to ask for a backstory. I like that.

I was living alone, doing odd jobs and making it work. I was coming to an understanding that in order to live this life, I have to put God first. I didn't, but I knew I should.

I was seeing an old friend, but we were never an item. She hated her life, and I was beginning to actually enjoy mine. So I gave her some advice about how to change. Believe it or not, she took it and landed a job she was wanting really bad in an advertisement agency.

One day, as I drove down from Oklahoma to Texas to visit with my son, the phone rang. It's my brother, and he's out of prison. He's on parole, but he's out. I thought that was amazing, and I was happy for him. I knew in time decisions would have to be made on my part to help him. Then the presence came over me, and this time it spoke to my heart directly, not through Simon. "What are you willing to lose, to receive?" Very cryptic but very poignant at the same time, I thought.

The drive to go see my son seemed to take forever. Over and over, I thought about those cryptic words, and then pulling up the drive of the house of my son's mother, it hit me, the answer. I don't know if it was right, but it was my answer. I said, "I'm willing to lose it all to help someone who never had a chance to succeed to succeed the right way." Then I spent a perfect day with my son.

After that, I found myself talking to my brother, and I made plans that night to pick up and move back to Texas so I could be closer to my son and to help my brother. I needed to be a father, and I needed to be a brother. My son was the catalyst, and in the end, a brother's love is a brother's love.

Chapter 9

Scary are waters for those who don't swim.

The First Time I Spoke

❖

You know how sometimes people walk into your life, sometimes again, with no apparent reason? My decision to move back to Texas was not one of those times. I knew God interjected Himself and with a purpose. I had bought furniture when I moved to Oklahoma City, and I was burdened by having to pack it all up and move back to Texas. But this time I was prepared. When I understood this, I didn't take another step. I sat down and prayed. God, Simon, or the other presence, who knows, put it on my heart to call the fella I bought the furniture from and sell it back to him. Long shot, I thought. Then I joked with myself, "Tell Peter that."

I called the gentleman at the furniture store, and to my amazement, not only did he want it back, but he was also willing to pay me almost what I paid for it, if it was in good condition. Well, my father taught me long ago to respect not only people, but also the things God lets you *borrow*. To my surprise, he sent his guys to go pick it up, free of charge. It was a 360 win. Touchdown Jesus. I said goodbye to Oklahoma City and found myself back in Texas.

My brother was a felon, and for felons, it's nearly impossible for them to get a place to lay their head. Enter stage left...me. My brother and I settled into a nice-sized two-bedroom apartment. We treated each other's space with respect. He didn't drink. I did, and he was cool with that. Often we would talk about the past, but he was more interested in the future. Shortly after we moved in together, I distinctly knew God was at work. Speaking of work, my brother landed a good job and began paying bills and getting established at a breakneck pace. He would tell me how he was getting the credit right and he was making plans to own some land and his house someday. All the while, he was courting a young lady in Tennessee. I was proud of him, and for maybe the first time in my life, my big brother was being, well, my big brother.

It wasn't long before Johnny Law would come knocking at my door. I was arrested yet again. This time it didn't even faze me. Ever hear of trumped-up charges? Well, that was my situation, and at that moment, sitting in county, I remembered a conversation with Doctor Victor. He asked how many times I had been arrested, and then he dropped some knowledge I never thought I'd hear a doctor say. I'm paraphrasing, "Victor, each time you've been arrested, you were drinking."

I thought, "Okay, here we go, blame the booze."

And then he continued with "Is drinking the culprit? Let's see. Unless you *only* drink when other people came around, and then things got bad, I would blame the alcohol. But how many times have you gone to jail drinking by yourself?"

I thought, and I answered truthfully, "Twice."

He snapped back, "I know, that was rhetorical, I'm staring at your file." He continued, "My point—you drink beer, not hard alcohol. I do think you have a 'drinking problem.'" He added, "But I believe you have more of a people problem." He was right. Those other two times I was arrested were for public intoxication.

So as I sat there at the county jail, it didn't faze me. I made a promise to God that I am never going to put myself in this situation, and God revealed to me how I got here and how to not let it happen again. I learned in that cell that the people I was surrounding myself with were the toxic ones. The only reason I kept them around was I didn't want to be alone. Time to cut sling load. (military jargon) No charges came from this arrest, but more insight than ever prevailed.

I started keeping busy and with good right. I was walking aimlessly, mind you, but at least I was moving. I was spending time with my son, and I was trying to be a father to my second daughter. Horrible rumors about me and her mother were making that a slow go. In short, I was getting nowhere fast with my daughter, but my relationship with my son was blossoming.

Then one day, without warning or a pretense, my son's mother said she doesn't want me in their life anymore. That shook me to the core, and at the time, there was nothing I could do. I had been arrested three times, I was an alcoholic, and I had a violent past in the eyes of the law. I knew it was a black-and-white thing from the jump. No, not race, but the typing of the words that the law was reading from my "own achievements" in the life. Then add doctor reviews into the mix for a child custody case, I would lose from the word go. So I did what I knew how to do. I offered child support and offered to leave them alone.

After that, my drinking surprisingly didn't take an uptick. I was on an even field. I was reading the Bible and listening to the universe. I wasn't trying to go out. I was focused internally, all the while talking to God. I didn't know where I was going, but I knew that journey inward would take me to the brink. I was thirty-three years old, and it was time I got to know me.

I would read and learn and be confused all at the same time. One minute, I knew the secret to life, but the next, I couldn't find my car keys for two days. I was still seeing a doctor for my PTSD, and I was still taking my medications. But something in me was waking up. The more I was waking up, the lesser Simon was there, but the other presence was growing stronger. Have you ever had random questioning thoughts? I.e., someone would cut me off in traffic, but instead of cussing up a storm, it was a question put on my heart. "How does that make you feel?" it would ask.

"Like I want to smack him in the face," I would think.

Although the question still lingered, and for the question to go away, I had to learn to do something that was taught to us in first grade. I had to use my words and confess out loud how it made me feel. The more I used my words, I found, the faster the process of seeing clearly would come about.

Before I knew it, every little thought of discontent I had, I was describing to myself how it made me feel. In turn, I was explaining to my heart and mind how my soul felt so my body could understand the reaction. Even in relationships, I was doing this so people could understand my actions, and believe it or not, as I explained this to them in the present, it spoke for itself of my actions in the past. It was so paradoxical, and it still is, to see them seeing and understanding for the first time why I have done the things I have done. I was seeing for the first time how the future could be great just by using words. I felt like a thirty-something man-child. For the first time in my life, I spoke with purpose.

Chapter 10

All is impossible. Divide it among those willing to challenge, and then you have I'm possible. That's the power of something higher.

A Gypsy with a Heart

❖━━━❖

The months passed, and my brother had found a way to stand on his own two feet. He was now engaged to a short firecracker of a woman from Tennessee. They were perfect for each other. My brother drowned himself in work, and she taught him how to enjoy the fruit of his labor. She knew about his past, and she didn't care. Slowly, she and I became friends, and she understood why I drank, which was to slow myself down.

I helped my brother on a down payment on a new truck. Wildly enough, I was in the market for a new car. He had told me about this place he went to, the people were super nice, and they had a gorgeous vice president. I was in an on-again-off-again kind of relationship that was off again. So I went to the dealership, and that's when I met Rosie. She. Was. Gorgeous. And I didn't want to move on her because my life wasn't quite straightened out yet. So instead, we would flirt.

I was in a relationship, but like I said, it was off again. That presence was ever so close. I knew change was coming. I felt like I was being used, and I had to make a move. My brother had moved out, and I was alone and not happy in the relationship I was in. It was time for another change. I threw away most of my things, and I was back on the road.

I drove back to the East Coast to spend time with my mother and to dry out a bit. I helped her around the house, and we spoke about life, love, and death. My mother put reflection back into my heart. She would regale me and anyone who would listen to embarrassing stories about her baby boy. She spoke fondly of one of the officers she knew and loved, who was killed in the line of duty. She cried. I cried. Before long, I was a rambling man again, driving all the way to the West Coast in a car that Rosie sold me. She was amazed when I didn't test drive it when I bought it. Still trying to impress her, I said confidently, "Her test drive would be on the open highway." As I was driving off, I was pleading with the car not to let me down. It didn't.

I traveled along the Rockies. The mountaintops were as high as any drink or dream can take you. I was in heaven, and I made it all the way to Cheyenne and sat outside that night and just stared at the stars. My life was catching up with me because I was slowing down and starting to finally live it. The presence was there, and it was drawing closer. I hadn't heard from Simon, but I knew wherever he was, he was keeping a watchful eye.

I made it to Washington State to pay my respects to my friend who had passed in Afghanistan. I made it to the gates of the cemetery but no further. I felt that I could do this, visit his grave, another time. I drove off and said a prayer for him and asked him to say a prayer for me. This trip was different. Though peaceful, it seemed purposeless. I was missing something, and at the bar of the hotel where I was staying, the purpose found me.

One chilly night in Washington State, I was having a bad time. I was having thoughts of hurting myself, and I had to pull myself from the brink. It seemed, I was wondering aimlessly in my life. "No one cares," my mind would race.

All the while, I was telling myself exactly what I should do. That night, in that hotel room, I was fighting something. It wasn't the presence I was used to. This thing was pushing me mentally to break the routine. It felt like a physical, mental fight, and it wanted me to hit that wall. I hit it and slit my wrist at the same time. In short, this was the fight I was preparing for.

"The hardest opponent is the man in the mirror," said Rocky Balboa, and for me, the greatest victim is a kind heart that can't love on its own terms. I was hurting mentally because I couldn't help others physically. What was missing on this trip? A Charlie, someone I could actually help. In my heart of hearts, helping others had been my saving grace all this time. If I hadn't been conceived, my mother probably would have stayed with my father just for the great job. Who knows how that would have turned out? If I hadn't helped Charlie, he was so trusting someone would've taken advantage of him.

Just a few examples of my life, my purpose was to help others, and that night it all rang clear. This whole time of running like a madman, I was still touching people's lives with my kindness. That's how I knew this presence wasn't bad because it put it on my heart to do so. All those miles and no car troubles? Really? I can't pick them that good, but somehow I got to where I was going with no hiccups. The only hiccup was my own train of thought.

I called Rosie from Washington State the next day. I asked her for $400 and a couch to sleep on. She wired the money, and forty-eight hours later, I was at her door. It was partially out of convenience, but it was mostly because I trusted her. She had no judgments on me. All this while, while being a fixture on her couch, I was still spending time with my brother and sister and father, and things were running smoothly. I decided to donate money that I received from a settlement, and I decided it was about time that I be a decent human being.

On the outside, I was a cool put-together guy. On the inside, it was torment because I knew I could do more, and that presence was urging me on to make some good things happen. It was almost an addiction. I wouldn't let myself want, per se, unless it benefited people who needed. Something snapped inside of me for the good when I was around Rosie. This was the push I needed to be a better man.

I was on nine different medications, and I wondered could these be affecting my thinking. "Well yeah" was put on my heart. So I did research. I decided to try marijuana, not to get high but to look at the most effective way I could use it to my benefit. It was a matter of months that the medications dropped. First one I dropped, Lithium, and me wanting to do that even more was because I met a pharmacist who happened to be a Christian, and she told me that all these meds, plus the beer, were killing me. Time for a change.

Shortly after, I dropped to six medications. Now I was down to three, and one of them is for blood pressure. I refused narcotics for the pain I had, but it was my mind that I had to wrangle.

After I started tapering down, emotions ran high. Not violence, sadness, because the state of the world I was seeing with all is magnificence, it was stunning. But I also saw the bad with grand clarity, and that saddened me, to tears at times. I felt my soul was reaching out of my chest, and I wanted to fix the world. Then that presence was on full and strong. I had seen a lot, I was a gypsy, and my heart ached for the downtrodden.

The presence put it on my heart with this Bible verse, "Drive out demons, raise the dead and cure the sick, for as freely you receive as freely give," and a gypsies with a heart was born.

Chapter 11

Hate not the wrong done onto you, embrace yet the fierce flame that
is in your name. Use the heat to cozy your walls, for with God, when
those "enemies" become stranded, at least you can keep them warm.

Missing My Friend

The courtship between Rosie and I was inevitable. I was more on target in my life than I had ever been. For once, not only was I speaking with purpose, but I was also living with purpose. It was a new light on a withered flower. I would cook her dinner while she was at work. We would eat, and I would walk her to her room, kiss her on the cheek good night, and go reside on her couch. We split the bills, and we were living. I loved her, and she loved me.

The months passed, and I was still being a conversationalist with God, Simon, and the other presence. Everything I was doing was somehow helping others. I enjoyed that. I had a winning formula going, and I didn't want to lose it. I proposed to Rosie around her birthday. She accepted, and we planned on a wedding. I would've been content with a justice of the peace. She wasn't going for that. This wedding was her new adventure, and it was just in her nature. She caused me to think bigger while attempting to think deeper. So I did. I invited my best friend, not to be my best man,

I already had one, but just to be there. Will was his name, and just like his name, he had a tremendous amount of it.

Will and I met in the US Army when I was seventeen years old. My biological brother, for most my life, was in prison. So when I met Will, he became like a big brother. He gave me advice that would move my life. He was the coolest guy, someone I wanted to be like that was the ignition in my life, the will. When I was picking out my job for the military, he told me to make sure I pick something that if I transfer out of service, I could use the trade taught to me to find employment.

He showed up for the wedding, and it was seamless how our friendship continued, even down to the fight we almost got into at the bar at my impromptu bachelor party. That's another story for another time. Rosie and my wedding went off without a hitch. All her friends, the dress, the mood were all perfect. My father wasn't there.

The months leading up to the wedding found my father and I at odds about things that happened in the past, not in my childhood, but adulthood. Horrible rumors still surrounded me. But what I have learned is If it wasn't for the bitterness of those who really don't matter but hate me, then the sweetness of those who love me would go unappreciated.

With all the arrests and all the stories, my father believed I was a violent man. But the people in my life who mattered knew differently. Rosie knew different, and that's all that mattered.

At the wedding, standing there were people whom I knew loved me and would take a lightning strike for me. I felt God, Simon, and just beyond the crowd, just beyond the sound of the claps and the glow of the distant candles, the presence. But that day, the presence became clearer in my mind's eye, a "planets aligning" moment, not perfect, but I felt that he was a guide.

The presence was silent, mentally visual, but I never felt the "conversation" until later, but I felt at peace standing at the altar. All our friends shared this moment, but being surrounded by love, and with the love of my life, I still missed my friend, my roadie, my copilot, and my navigator. I still missed my go-to-no-matter-what-I-was-going-through. I missed my father, and I'm not ignorant enough to pretend I don't. My prayers prove I still do.

Chapter 12

Take another's hand. Is not the warmth of another's spark worth a
thousand suns? Is not a grain of hope worth your coat in cold fear?

The Revival

———————◆•◆•◆———————

My new bride and I made our way down to my godparents' house in East Texas. John and Evelyne, hardworking people, were down home. They both worked for the city for over twenty years each. They lived a fast life until some years ago. They gave their heart fully to the Lord. The Lord had taken John through a time to which John feared he wouldn't come out the other side. Evelyn, still the rock she was, proved to be John's shoreline. After that, they became a beacon for those lost souls who made their way through life's fog and to the lighthouse that was their door. They were sanctuary from the wolves and cold, and they were fair.

Giving their time, and in many cases like first my brother, and then later-myself, they gave room and board. My brother reached out to John during one of his many prison stints. I met John and Evelyn the last time my brother was released, and we all became fast friends. I was reminded later that John and I had met sometime before. I didn't remember. John drank like I did, and he and I thought on the same level. We spent many a night discussing God, the heavens, and politics. Getting lost in conversation is the best way to explore the woods of the unknown, no direction, just the fire of curiosity leading the way. They were just great people to be around.

Evelyne and John were regular parishioners and pastors at a church in East Texas. I had gone to the church to watch Arron, the preacher, preach. I have faith and have for a long time. And I'm still skeptical of how others define the "bar" of their faith, but Arron was different. He seemed genuine. Very powerful is not an accurate-enough description of the energy that surrounded this man. In one Sunday school with young adults, he played an Eminem song, not the censored version, at the church. He wasn't critical of the song; he offered a different look at it.

Arron spoke with a Southern draw and was a young man in comparison to the Southern Baptist, Protestant, and Catholic churches I have been to. He was married and had a child, and before God touched his heart, Arron was a drug dealer. He drank and swore, and he knew he was on the wrong road. Arron knew that he was living in the world and not in the word. How he became saved and let his heart to Jesus, well, to be honest, I don't know the whole backstory. I just know the passion and fierceness that followed, which was now the church.

His different look at Eminem's song was simple. He gave Eminem the credit for being a great poet; it just wasn't Arron's type of poetry. Then Arron said, "If Eminem would produce a gospel rap with the same fire, he would reach so many more fans."

Let's face it: Marshall Mathers has millions of fans. Now if you were to flip just a small percentage of those fans who weren't "saved," what a tidal wave that would be? But this is how Arron spoke. I took time to figure what he meant by that. It's like the words you are reading. *Anyone* could write these words, but an example is greater than any instruction.

My wife and I spent the weekend in East Texas with my godparents. It was peaceful and productive. We chewed the fat over the word and the world. It's hard to survive one without the other. We made it to church revival that Saturday night. The church was a deep one room hall, enough to fill 160 people at capacity. On this night, it was just about fifty people, and the service was about three hours long. As the service was wrapping up, the presence showed up, and this time I wasn't the only one to feel it. Arron called me to the front row, and he spoke to me in front of everyone. He knew I had back trouble from an incident that happened overseas. He knew I had been in psychological and physical turmoil for most of my adult life. He knew I was tired, and he knew I was in pain.

He knew I was coming to an end of a long road, and God knew I needed to hear his words. We prayed in the front for all to see. I always kept the conversations between me and God private.

Arron asked with compassion and confidence, "You have lower-back pain?" And then he suddenly stopped and spoke in tongues for a moment and retorted, "Terrible back pain." He asked with certainty, "Do you want to give it to God?"

I thought, "Hell yeah!"

I wasn't taking any narcotics, and at this time in my life, I was down to less medications than before I had to start taking them. To say the least, I was in pain and I needed to give it away.

As Arron was talking to me, and I was talking to God, something found its way around me, and the emotion was more powerful than anything I've ever felt. That presence was coming alive in me. Arron touched my lower back and began to pray. He asked God to remove the lower-back pain from me. That was where the pain had resided for years. If you knew me longer than six months, you knew that at one point I would be incapacitated by pain. That day changed my life.

"God, I ask you to take his lower-back pain and throw it away," Arron continued.

As Arron touched my lower back, he prayed for it to rise. Arron said that God wanted the pain to rise to the upper back, and the rest was up to me. The pain would resemble a caterpillar who had yet to receive his wings. In terms, I hadn't reached a certain point of metamorphoses. The reason to bring the pain higher was to serve as a reminder for me to keep moving, to keep striving for what seems out of reach.

I've seen Arron many times give accurate predictions to people lives, and now he was predicting mine. He spoke of not only the next journeys in my life, but also the journeys of my new bride. Arron's faith was so strong, and his faith reassured my faith. That is the kind of fellowship I needed. When I walked in, I was on crutches in faith, but being there in that church that night, my faith got stronger. I knew Arron was just a translator for something that my eye couldn't see. I felt like there was something in that church that was in direct concert with God, something truly paranormal. This was the real deal.

I had been saved before, when I was a child, when I was in Iraq, and when I was in Alaska. All this time, I didn't know if it stuck, but this night reassured me, unlike it had from the first time. My mind rang clear for the first time in forever. I cried tears of anguish for the past wrongdoings I had done. I believe my wife was crying for all the wrongdoings done to me, and the presence of God was crying tears of joy for the next strides my life will take.

Arron predicted great things for my family. He prayed for *all* my family without retention. Looking back, it felt like a graduation, a higher perspective to allow me to see the bigger picture. But amazingly enough, the bigger picture had nothing to do with what the eyes see or how the heart feels. It was how my soul knew. Call it instinct, a gut feeling, or hope, but I knew that it was right then and there that the real work had to start. All I wanted to do, all my life, even before I knew helping folks was my addiction, and my saving grace. I'm not rich, but I have wealth in God. I'm not perfect, but I serve a perfect God. I'm not done, and God is not done with me or *you*.

If helping Charlie or my brother was like staring at the moon, then this night I was walking on a sun that had been found in a black hole while in a rain forest over a flourishing garden. That is how that moment felt. I knew then that I knew nothing. It was all faith all along. I did know one thing when I walked out of that church, that my next days were to be with purpose.

Chapter 13

Hope in the smoke will be too late. We are here.

Roll On (Taken out of Time)

———◆———

There is something honest about an honest failure, after giving your all and it still isn't enough. My life, for a long time, was an honest failure. So I thought. I would constantly compare myself with others and never be satisfied with what God had set for me or how He set me up to be, which is myself.

It's like the meme "Don't compare your chapter 1 to someone else's chapter 20." So much truth to that in so little words. After the revival, I took a really long look at my life and how life took me through curves and swerves without so much as an apology. Life sometimes can be a cool or cruel partner, but it is always teaching us something. And I think the moment you stop trying to learn is the moment it starts to end.

Through all the ups and downs, plans and letdowns, I find it funny how this life can still make me smile. As I write these words, Kobe Bryant passed away five months ago. Coronavirus and protest are all over this great nation, and we still have six months left in this year. Even though it's hard to see the good in life these days, you can still find it if you look close enough. It's in the news report of the old man who still comes and visits his wife every day in the nursing home through glass, and every mile he walked, he picked a couple of wild flowers because his dad thought him to never show up empty-handed. Or the newborn baby who spent seven weeks in ICU because of Covid-19 but made a full and awesome recovery. Or my daughter's mother who allowed our daughter to stay with me extra time because school was cancelled for the year. Life is awesome in its own little way. There were so many people in my life I had to let go because I was trying to better myself and they wanted to stay in the same spot. No, I'm not better than them. I just got tired of my own excuses.

So as 2020 rolls on, I wrote a book. I figured it was now or never. I had the time, and I had the story. And if you are on a runaway train just hold on tight. I am confident I am not alone on this journey. And maybe you've felt the same way. All I do know, wishing for hope in the smoke, will be too late. What could've been is probably already destroyed. So like what Nike says, just do it. You never know, you might even surprise the greatest miracle, that is the person in the mirror. Reading these words, thank you from the bottom of my heart for the opportunity to give you a glimpse of my life. And if you're on the fence about anything in life that will make you better, please don't think about it too long. Before you know it, a year and then another year will go by, and you will more than likely miss the opportunity to make a difference, a difference not only in your life, but also in a complete stranger's life, maybe even mine.

The sun will rise tomorrow. Every storm runs out of rain. Sometimes life can be the tranquility of a newborn baby's cry or the chaos of a runaway freight.

Chapter 14

Does not a circle meet itself?

Enter Jack

———————◆◆◆———————

To this day, that day with my wife, Arron, and my godparents is still a driving force. After that night, I felt that Simon had taken a back seat, and this presence was now a force that was becoming stronger. It wasn't clear at first where this was going to lead. But it is becoming clearer every day. In recent prayer, I have listened with my soul what the universe is speaking.

I speak more kindly to people I don't know. I understand that the sun doesn't revolve around me, but life revolves around love. I know now that this life is meant to be lived, in depth and not watched as it passes you by. I realized I rather go broke helping others than live in a mansion with rooms I don't need standing vacant. I had to submit so many times because my pride built me up so high, and it was false hope with little faith. I knew that all those roads I took led me to write these pages and will lead me to the morning sun feeling a bit more accomplished.

I called Simon his name since I was a child because he said that's what his name was. But this presence, at first didn't have a name. I meditated and prayed and spoke out loud to this presence. And it was only recently the presence put it on my heart to "translate" what he was showing my soul. So I began writing this memoir. What are some of the things he has shared with me? I will share them with you. Reread these last words and the words in italic are the words of this presence and the points of life he has revealed to me. By the way, he said for me to call him Jack.

After that, and until this day, I still don't speak to my father. But my brother, sister, and mother are as close as can be. Just recently, something happened that is hard to explain. This, I believe, is the purpose for these writings. Just recently, it was put on my heart that what I'm looking for is "beyond the scope of my bubble." All the words you have read so far was written within twelve hours. The next part of this story takes place within the last four days.

Some weeks ago, my service dog was sitting on the couch in the middle of the night. I had to go to the bathroom, and I saw him staring at nothing, but something was there. I felt it. I said a prayer and thought nothing of it. This continued many nights until my wife had taken him out for his morning walk, and she said something spooked him. My dog is still a puppy, but he is mostly calm. This day his hair stood on end, and he hurried back into the house. This is the first time I'm saying or writing this, but the night before my dog was spooked, the presence put it on my heart he wanted to talk.

I meditated, and thoughts that are hard to explain came to my mind. And the feeling of peace and understanding followed. This presence was now letting me hear its thoughts on life and love.

"Answers to questions are innate, I live within the foolish. All you have to do is ask." That is one quote out of many. And I'm writing this because it was put on my heart to "tell a story." My story is no better than anyone else's. But maybe my story will help others.

The point to all this is not to give up. This life is worth it. Every tear, every moment is ours to embrace and hold on to as long as we can. At the end, "Does not a circle meet itself? So is our reunion."

The end.

CPSIA information can be obtained
at www.ICGtesting.com
Printed in the USA
LVHW040441230122
709146LV00005B/306